A L E S S I

C U T T I N G   E D G E

FAY SWEET

ALESSI

Art and Poetry

WATSON
GUPTILL

First published in 1998 in the United States of America by
Watson-Guptill Publications, a division of
Billboard Publications, Inc.,
1515 Broadway, New York, NY 10036

Library of Congress CIP data applied for.

ISBN 0-8230-1145-3

This book was conceived, designed, and produced by
THE IVY PRESS LTD
2/3 St Andrew's Place
Lewes, East Sussex BN7 1UP

Art director: TERRY JEAVONS
Design and page layout: ALAN OSBAHR
Commissioning editor: CHRISTINE DAVIS
Managing editor: ANNE TOWNLEY

Printed in Hong Kong

Contents

"**A**lessi is not a normal factory. I think of it as an applied arts research laboratory. We have devised a unique system of harnessing the talent of the world's most interesting designers; we call them maestros, and encourage them to make use of and stretch our technical expertise. We want them to push our knowledge to the extreme. Alessi's role is to mediate between the most interesting expressions of creativity of our times and the dreams of the consumer. We like to lead where others follow. Some of our objects are so extraordinary no other manufacturer would consider making them; it is a risk to put them into production, but if the design feels right, I have no hesitation in going ahead. The possibilities of creativity are immense, and we have no limit on what we can do. For us, design is an artistic and poetic discipline."

Alberto Alessi

Introduction

CLOSE TO MILAN CATHEDRAL, in the famous shopping avenue of Corso Matteotti, there is one store window that never fails to attract the eye. Whether stacked high with glinting stainless steel or crowded with colorful plastic, the Alessi store is always full of intrigue. The products on display are undoubtedly some of the most innovative to have made their way into our homes this century. From kettles and cafetières to toilet brushes and bottle stoppers, they have significantly transformed the way we think about ordinary household goods.

The objects themselves are produced in the Italian Alps, just outside the small town of Crusinallo, some 100kms (60 miles) northwest of Milan. Here, after threading through the narrow streets at the heart of town, the road opens along a river valley bound for Lake Orta. The riverbanks are dotted with businesslike gray factories turning out pots, pans, and kitchen utensils as they have done for decades. Sky-high mountains supply a dramatic backdrop; in the 17th century men would cross these mountains, following the "Pewter Road," to find employment in German metal workshops. When they returned, they brought their new skills with them. A local metalworking tradition developed and a sense of proud heritage and continuing tradition is still tangible today. But there's a rebel in town, someone who refuses to do things like they've always been done. Visitors will have spotted the first clue to his existence back in the center where a massive blue plastic woman stands guard outside a storage depot. And the game is given away on the outskirts of Crusinallo on arriving at a neat collection of red, yellow, blue, and green buildings—this time featuring an oversized teapot—which bear the nameplate Alessi.

Despite its unorthodox appearance, Alessi is a venerable member of the local industrial fraternity. The company was founded in 1921 at nearby Omegna by Giovanni Alessi, paternal grandfather of Alberto Alessi. With its expertize in lathe-turning brass and nickel silver, Alessi's first products included coffeepots, serving dishes, and trays for the hotel and catering trade. In 1928 the company moved to the current site where it continues to make and sell many of those early designs.

The manufacture of metal kitchenware was also pursued locally by another branch of the family. In the 1930s Alfonso Bialetti, Alberto Alessi's maternal grandfather, invented, designed, and began to manufacture the octagonal, cast-aluminum coffee maker, the Bialetti Moka Express. It has since become a classic and continues to be produced to this day.

The young Alberto was fascinated by these two very different workshops. He recalls: "At one extreme there was the mechanized Bialetti production line, turning out its single coffeepot design by the thousand, and then there was Alessi that employed skilled craftsmen to carry out labor-intensive lathe work, detailing, and polishing for a range of beautifully finished objects. When I

From left: the original Alessi factory around 1935;
the modern factory in a quirky advertisement from 1995;
Carlo Alessi with the Bombé tea and coffee service.

started working in the company in 1970 I wanted to combine the strengths of the two types of workshops, making mass production and craftsmanship work together."

Alberto was later joined by other members of the third generation of Alessis: his brothers Michele and Alessio, and cousin Stefano. The company has since undergone something of a metamorphosis. It has something of a dual personality; the classic hotel and restaurant lines continue to be produced, but better known to the international design audience is its range of household objects created by many of the legends of 20th-century style.

The roll call is impressive: there's Philippe Starck, Ettore Sottsass, Achille Castiglioni, Michael Graves, Aldo Rossi, Alessandro Mendini, and Richard Sapper to name a few. These are the Alessi "maestros," each testing ideas and working on innovative new products that often develop into entire collections.

Responsible for encouraging and harnessing this vast body of talent is Alberto Alessi, who acts as catalyst and conductor for this orchestra of designer—performers. Building on the creative ideals of schools such as the Bauhaus and collaborative groups of artists and designers like the Weiner Werkstätte (Vienna Workshops), Alberto Alessi had always intended to make the company a laboratory for new thought and a crucible for forging innovative ideas. "Alessi is a company that makes design," he says. "We are not an industrialist in the classic sense of the term, but rather a kind of research and development workshop, or laboratory, operating in the applied arts. Our role is to act as a mediator between the designer and the needs and dreams of the market."

Along with design, Alberto Alessi's most enduring passions are philosophy and psychology. His training, however, was in law. His designer father, Carlo, who between 1935 and 1945 created some of Alessi's best-selling lines, and who thereafter became general manager, initially did not want his son to follow in his footsteps; preferring him to have "a solid, professional job." But when the time came, Alberto took up the reins. He recalls: "Sales to the hotel and catering trade were good… but where was the challenge?"

The maestros

Many preferring a quiet, predictable life would have held the company on a steady course, but Alberto Alessi was hungry for experiment. "I wanted to make changes, to have some fun. No one can imagine how boring it can be to run a factory. And I was very lucky right from the beginning to have the opportunity to work with clever, creative people." He first asked his architect friend Franco Sargiani and the Finnish graphic designer Eija Helander to work on the design of a range of stainless steel tableware. Part of the brief was to create adaptable and flexible forms that would enhance the food they contained, and that would use table space efficiently. The resulting modular system,

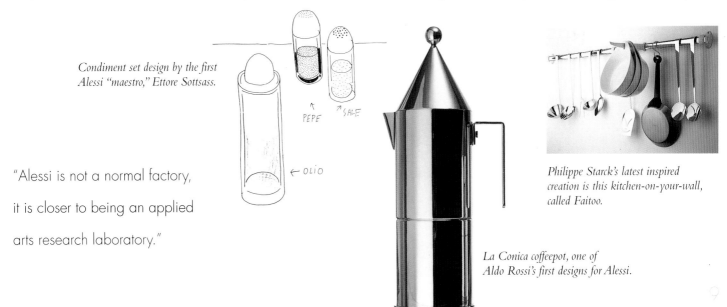

Condiment set design by the first Alessi "maestro," Ettore Sottsass.

PEPE SALE

OLIO

"Alessi is not a normal factory,

it is closer to being an applied

arts research laboratory."

Philippe Starck's latest inspired creation is this kitchen-on-your-wall, called Faitoo.

La Conica coffeepot, one of Aldo Rossi's first designs for Alessi.

incorporating square and rectangular trays and vessels, was radical in many ways—it used steel in its own right and not as a substitute for more expensive materials, its shape was unlike any other, it was aimed at a domestic market, and it acknowledged that younger professional consumers were living in apartments and small homes where space was at a premium.

The collaboration continued until the end of the 1970s and Sargiani suggested Alessi might for future projects commission other designers—perhaps the great Ettore Sottsass. "I had long been an admirer of Sottsass' work and this was a wonderful opportunity to meet and work with a hero," recalls Alessi. The two started talking about designs for some trays, but eventually resolved to focus on a project for a condiment set. It took four years in the making and remains one of the company's all-time best-sellers. Sottsass became the first Alessi maestro.

In answer to the frequent questions about how the maestro relationship works, Alberto Alessi describes himself as "the receiver and transmitter of their ideas." He explains: "Each maestro brings their own philosophy and working techniques. Richard Sapper and Aldo Rossi, for example, are drawn from entirely different design traditions, but each is respected for his method of working. Sapper is from the tradition of the German Ulm School, the successor of the Bauhaus, where designers were expected to know about manufacturing technology, and so he

takes a prominent role in the production process. Aldo Rossi is not interested in detail—he is concerned with the integrity of the concept and expects the technicians to use their expertise to make things work. And then there are designers like Philippe Starck who work at the same time in broad conceptual sweeps and with minute attention to the detail of a handle, say, or a lid."

By pursuing creativity and innovation first, in advance of economic or technical considerations, Alessi is a rare beast indeed. The very notion is heady stuff in an age when industry is obsessed with market forces, overheads, and turnover. But Alberto Alessi is determined to propagate a new way of working: "Our philosophy does not put economics or mass production first. The traditional factory conceives design as a tool for marketing and technology, but we disagree totally. We think of design as an artistic and poetic discipline."

The design factory in Crusinallo aims to foster this creative spirit. In the model-making workshops and prototype rooms, shelves and tables are stacked high with intriguing and ever-more flamboyant objects. Hundreds of projects sit here taking shape— a prototype aluminum bicycle is on the workbench awaiting further work on detail, a scatter of brightly colored plastic trays has just been completed, and print quality is being checked for the latest oven gloves, dish towels, and aprons. Only a small percentage of these objects might ever make it to the stores.

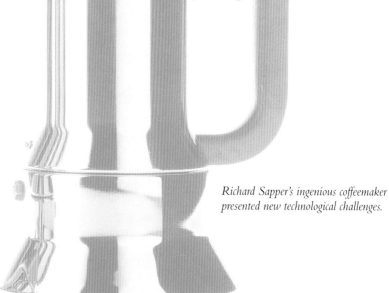

Richard Sapper's ingenious coffeemaker presented new technological challenges.

Theory of the Borderline

The process of selecting projects to be prototyped rests with Alberto Alessi. Choices are based largely on his intuitive knowledge of what will appeal to the people. However, he also draws on philosophy and his own "Theory of the Borderline."

"The borderline is about risk," says Alberto Alessi. "One of our distinguishing characteristics is that we choose to work very close to the borderline. This line marks what people find intriguing and appealing and will buy, from what leaves them unmoved and therefore remains on the shelf. If you work too far away from the borderline it is disastrous. For example in car production, where no risks are taken, all cars grow to look the same and the market becomes deadened."

Adding piquancy to the borderline is the fact that that it cannot be seen. "You can feel it, almost smell it, but it is not clearly drawn—and it keeps moving," says Alessi. And there are perils associated with treading too close to the edge—you can lose your footing and fall. This produces what Alberto Alessi calls a "fiasco," a product that is just too far away from what the consumer will accept. Alberto views these fiascos in a positive light, however. "As you fall on the other side your way is lit for an instant by a flash of bright light. For one second it's possible to clearly see where the borderline is, and this can prove very helpful for other projects." One of the company's most famous fiascos is the Hot Bertaa kettle by Philippe Starck, a curious Viking's helmet-shaped vessel speared with a pipe for handle and spout. "I love it, even if it doesn't work well and if at the end of the day we sell it only to what Starck calls 'my design victims.' It is precious to me because it gave me such a clear vision of the borderline. Most satisfying of all is when I know we have succeeded in moving the borderline. This is my idea of progress."

Formula for Success

In a bid to understand the fiasco and the best-seller, Alberto Alessi has devised a highly individual "Formula for Success." This identifies the components that trigger our reactions to objects.

He took the past as his starting point. "I collected all the data on the lives of products made since my arrival in 1970 and then established some parameters by which to judge them. The first was the notion of 'sensoriality, memory, and imagination' or SMI. This provides a way of explaining what people mean when they say 'oh, what a beautiful object,' This is all about our very personal relationship with an object—is it pleasing to the senses, does it spark the imagination, does it stir emotions?" In Alberto's formula the SMI category is divided into five graded responses, from the "unpleasant" to the "exciting." A large number of Alessi products achieved the two highest marks, but it was still unclear what distinguished best-sellers from the rest.

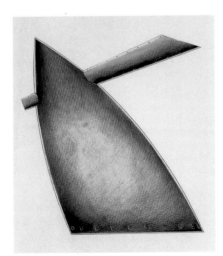

Starck's Hot Bertaa kettle: fiasco or the future?

"Some of our objects are so extraordinary no other manufacturer would consider making them; but if the design feels right, I have no hesitation in going ahead."

So Alberto then devised a category based on the idea of communication and language. This examines how we use objects as a form of expression. An object could be awarded one of five grades, from "out" (for the obsolete or kitsch) to "illuminating" (for products with cult status). A further two components were added: price and function. Some items might score well as sensual communication tools and perform less well on price and function. "Of course there are those who will dismiss the idea," says Alberto Alessi, "but we have found it invaluable, particularly as an evolved language for discussing projects in meetings. The terms help to explain the appeal of designs and the reasons for taking them into production. The system even helps in selecting appropriate designers. For example if I'm developing a product where price is shown to be important then I know who not to approach."

Beyond the millennium

Among the highest scores for success in the late 1990s is the Alessi plastic tableware. Two of the best-sellers are the Lilliput magnetic salt and pepper set by Stefano Giovannoni and the brightly colored napkin rings by Mattia Di Rosa as well as Alessandro Mendini's "Anna G" corkscrew. (It's a scaled-up Anna G figure that stands outside the Alessi depot in Crusinallo.) These objects mark a radical departure from the familiar Alessi fare, and to stalwart Modernists they are shockingly frivolous and even anti-Alessi. They are

proving enormously popular with young consumers, however. Alberto Alessi acknowledges that the introduction of plastic has caused a few raised eyebrows. "At the beginning we had strong reactions from people saying that by moving into plastic we were damaging the Alessi image, losing our identity, cheapening ourselves. My response to this conservatism is that far from losing our identity, we are helping to move it on and evolve."

The product portfolio has changed dramatically in the past decade—where once Alessi manufactured using only metal, it now incorporates glass, wood, ceramics, and plastics. "The decision to broaden our range of materials was taken because we wanted to extend the idea of Alessi as an applied arts laboratory," explains Alessi. "In the past our designers were limited to working in metal, but we felt it was time to open up the palette of materials and offer them more opportunities to express themselves. Plastics are particularly exciting, and there's room for such a lot of innovative work to be done here."

Alberto Alessi has no qualms about moving away from the strictness and simplicity of Modernism. "After all, Modernism is passed," he says with resounding finality. He is convinced that the Modernist credo stood between us and our deep relationship with products, suppressing our longing for color and texture and decoration. "Objects have a language and they speak to us, even if in unconscious ways and in different languages depending on

"The possibilities of creativity

are immense, and we have no limit

on what we can do. The challenge

is to stay ahead."

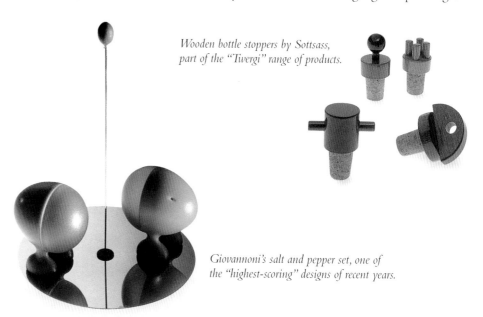

Wooden bottle stoppers by Sottsass, part of the "Tivergi" range of products.

Giovannoni's salt and pepper set, one of the "highest-scoring" designs of recent years.

the designers who create them. At Alessi we want to explore these languages; we are looking for the 'toyful,' the more expressive, more complex, and more delightful."

Much of the new thinking springs from Alberto Alessi's fascination with the work of psychoanalysts Franco Fornari and D.W. Winnicott. Fornari's theory suggests that our choices in life are predominantly ruled by emotion, while Winnicott identifies in human existence a need for toys and play to remind us of the happiness and security of childhood.

"In our deepest beings we respond to, and have an urgent need for childish objects," says Alessi. "Apparently uncomplicated, these kinds of objects give us pleasure and reassurance. Modernism temporarily purged us of these objects of enjoyment, but we are now ready for their return."

To experiment with these ideas, Alessi has established the Centro Studi, a design and philosophy workshop based in Milan. Involving young designers and students, the workshop's projects explore the roles and perceptions of objects. Leading designers and academics work alongside the teams. Among the first objects to emerge and enter production were the series of bowls, canisters, and plates with the enigmatic title Memory Containers. Following on from this has come the much larger sequence of products, mostly made in plastic, called Family Follows Fiction. "The intention here was to explore, to the very end of their possibilities, a number of expressive keys such as play, memory, and emotive involvement," explains Alessi.

As this line of thought continues, others are simultaneously being investigated. Currently preoccupying Alberto Alessi is the idea of the "thingness of things" and the statement "poetically lives the man." Both derive from the 1950s' writings of philosopher Martin Heidegger, and explore the notion of the ultimate essence of things, the merging of function with aesthetics. "If we take a kettle and really understand the kettleness of the kettle we should come close to knowing the real reasons for it to exist," says Alessi. "This could be functional, mystical, ritual, a combination of all three or something else entirely." Alessi refutes the suggestion that this is another version of the Modernist mantra of form follows function: "By incorporating the extra dimension of emotion, it is a great deal richer than its predecessor."

The body of work in this book is divided into collections or "metaprojects." These product families may be the work of one designer or may stem from a particular branch of research and exploration. The projects go beyond the usual concept of product design to embrace philosophy, cultural questioning, and research. Whether led by the maestros or emerging from the Centro Studi workshop, each metaproject is a new journey and a reflection of Alberto Alessi's concept of design as "an artistic and poetic discipline."

Designs from the Memory Containers project, initiated by the Centro Studi.

THE FATHER OF 20th-century Italian design, Ettore Sottsass was a fitting choice as the first Alessi maestro. His prodigious, and influential, output has included typewriters and office furniture for Olivetti; lighting for Artemide; telephones, ceramics, and glassware. In the 1960s he became a leading figure of the Anti-Design movement and then in the 1980s won international stardom when he led the Memphis design co-operative that caused a sensation with its kitsch-pop designs. Despite having celebrated his 80th birthday in 1997, Sottsass continues to question and innovate.

Sottsass' relationship with the company began in 1972 when Alberto Alessi invited him to design some new stainless steel trays. A long-time admirer of the Sottsass oeuvre, Alberto Alessi was also fascinated by his intellectual approach to design: "Ettore has considerable charm, he has exceptional, physical, mental, and creative strength, and he's a philosopher who is able to say interesting things about any subject."

Alberto Alessi has been deeply influenced by Sottsass' wisdom in discussing the role of industry. Early in their relationship Sottsass pointed out that Alessi had the power to change lives and influence culture with his products; it's an idea the company has actively pursued ever since. Sottsass also clearly revels in the stimulating working relationship they have forged during the past quarter of a century, and their joint quest to make the archetypal and indispensable. "We thought we could design products that were tools for existence rather than tools for the sake of being," he maintains.

The tray project was rapidly overtaken by a more complex challenge to produce a condiment set. The designs required considerable technical input and it was four years before they went on sale. However, the work has remained continuously in production ever since and is among the company's all-time best-selling items.

C O N D I M E N T   S E T
Ettore Sottsass, 1978

The first Sottsass project for Alessi was this elegant condiment set with containers for oil, vinegar, salt, pepper, and toothpicks. A Parmesan cheese cellar completes the ensemble.

P I A Z Z A   B A T T I S T A
Ettore Sottsass, 1989

The condiment set was later re-created in wood for the Twergi label. The base uses different colors of beech.

CONDIMENT SET
Ettore Sottsass, 1978

The condiment set's success must surely be attributed to the elegance and simplicity of its forms: smooth-sided glass cylinders with unadorned stainless steel domed caps. The classical proportions and perfection of the design make these deeply desirable objects. The shining crystal and metal is reminiscent of perfume holders, bestowing a sense of preciousness on the oil, vinegar, salt, and pepper they contain.

LA BELLA TAVOLA
Ettore Sottsass, 1993

In his **La Bella Tavola** series of porcelain tableware Sottsass experiments with form and applied decoration.

NUOVO MILANO
Ettore Sottsass, 1987

While it may look simple, this cutlery involved a long and complex development process. The **Nuovo Milano** won the XV Golden Compass award in 1989.

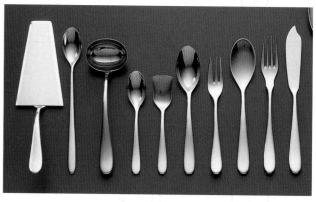

Place-setting detail. The seductively rounded forms of this cutlery fit perfectly in the hand. "I wanted to reach a zone where the design is purely tactile," says the designer.

GINEVRA
Ettore Sottsass, 1996

The sensuality of Sottsass' work is explored in glass in his Ginevra series. The decanter is extremely handsome with its unusually broad neck and simple, straight-sided body.

LA BELLA TAVOLA
Ettore Sottsass, 1993

The generously rounded forms of La Bella Tavola (opposite) are especially easy to appreciate when the tableware is seen together as a group. The design has an appealing serenity, and each piece invites the touch.

With a deep fascination for the ritual of eating, few people are better suited to designing tableware than Ettore Sottsass. Preparing a beautiful table is for Sottsass "a very graceful way of showing awareness, respect, and care about that basic event of having food. If there is a beautiful table where everything is neat and tidy, where everything's clean and all the tableware is carefully laid, you feel more like taking part in a ritual."

Sottsass went on to design a variety of diverse objects for Alessi—from a metal basket and bar accessories to the cutlery set Nuovo Milano (1987). The seductively rounded, fluid forms of the cutlery are enticingly tactile. This is exactly the reaction that Sottsass sought: "I wanted this cutlery to be of a classic and simple design that would have a special kind of magic when touched, that people would notice its design only when they handled it." His recent Ginevra glassware is generous and sensual too—but this time the bulbous forms are given a welcome edge of tension with the slightly outturned lip.

In his tableware, La Bella Tavola, Sottsass again appeals to our senses. Once again a lip is added, providing a striking contrast to the spherical shapes. It has three different finishes: a plain white, a pale blue zig-zag, and a broad multicolored band.

Richard Sapper

HE SECOND MAESTRO, and suggested by Sottsass, was Richard Sapper. His Alessi debut was made with the groundbreaking stainless steel espresso coffeemaker, the company's first product for the kitchen in decades.

The project's progress was slow at first because Sapper was "engaged in technological audacities," recalls Alessi. His unceasing quest for new ways of making the object tried the skills, and the patience, of the company's technicians. Nevertheless, the new coffeemaker eventually emerged—a sleek, high-tech, stainless steel vessel with a broad squat base rising to a slim cylinder with a flat top and a small, understated spout. That Sapper tested the Alessi technicians was only good news to Alberto Alessi; in subsequent projects he has actively encouraged the maestros to push materials and technology to their limits. "I can assure you that working on a project with Sapper is a tonic for industry," says Alberto. "In the end, though perhaps a little tired, it finds itself better, stronger, more innovative."

Sapper's adventures with the 9090 Coffeemaker were followed by the Kettle with a Singing Whistle (1983). This was what Alberto calls a poetic expedition, and one that led to the birth of the so-called "designer" kettle. Where once we had been content to boil our water in a variety of anonymous vessels, there was now the option of making hot water with beauty and music. Once again this fulfilled Alberto Alessi's vision of adding lyricism to everyday tasks.

Because existing kettles tend to let out such a piercing and unpleasant screech, Sapper's dream was to make a kettle that sang prettily. He wanted to re-create something from his childhood, the sound of riverboats he had heard as a young boy. Sapper's long search for the melodic two-tone whistle eventually took him to a craftsman in the Black Forest who made brass tuning pipes. The sound was eventually perfected and the brass whistle fitted to the spout.

9 0 9 0   C O F F E E M A K E R
Richard Sapper, 1979

Alessi's first espresso coffeemaker has won numerous awards for its ingenious design. Sapper's inventiveness pushed Alessi's manufacturing technology to its limits. The resulting design features a revolutionary hinged mechanism for locking the base to the coffee chamber— an improvement on traditional models that require two hands to unscrew the bottom from the top. First issued in polished stainless steel (opposite)**, it is also produced in a matte black silicone finish** (below)**.**

With its distinctive two-tone whistle and domed shape, the Kettle with a Singing Whistle *(below)* has become one of Alessi's best-selling products. The kettle was developed over a three-year period, with the whistle alone taking a year to perfect. The trigger mechanism in the handle *(opposite top)* allows the whistle to be pulled away from the spout when refilling.

Achille Castiglioni

THE DESIGNER'S PURPOSE is to stimulate curiosity, amusement, and affection," says the irrepressible Achille Castiglioni. His witty designs regularly pierce the pompousness often prevalent in the design world—but with serious intent: "Ultimately, design simply means designing. What counts is not so much the person designing the object, as the practical use that can be made of it."

Castiglioni first worked for Alessi in 1980 on exhibition designs. Alberto Alessi then visited this new maestro at his office in Milan to talk about further projects. "We started to discuss cutlery and Achille reached for his archives and came up with a few sketches, prototypes, and designs he had made in the 1950s with his brother Pier Giacomo," says Alessi. These formed the starting point of Dry, the company's first cutlery set, launched in 1982.

Alberto Alessi is a great admirer of the designer's work, his enthusiasm and eloquence. "I consider Castiglioni to be a great master," he proclaims, "curious about everything and with a great gift for irony and exceptional modesty, but able to design masterpieces." He also knows that Castiglioni works best when his imagination is fired. "There must always be a spark, which can be provoked by an innovation or a functional idea," says Alberto. "But he doesn't like a design brief that's too constricting. It is difficult to get him to work if the spark isn't there."

The "spark" for Castiglioni's oil and vinegar cruet was the wish to find the solution to an annoying problem. "The trouble with oil and vinegar cruets is the lid. When you take it off you never know what to do with it." The answer came with the use of a counterweight—as the oil or vinegar is poured, the little flat top lifts up and out of the way. It is simple and thoughtful and enormously enjoyable to use. It also answers Alberto Alessi's demand for innovation in everyday objects.

S P I R A L E
Achille Castiglioni, 1970

Elegant and practical, the Spirale ashtray has become an Alessi classic. The wire spiral allows ash to be flicked away easily.

A M I C I
Achille Castiglioni, 1996

The charming heart shapes of the multicolored Amici napkin rings form part of Castiglioni's recent and most exuberant output.

F R U I T B O W L
Achille Castiglioni, 1995

Standing on an aluminum base, this combined fruit bowl and colander has the air of an ancient vessel of offering.

OIL AND
VINEGAR CRUET
Achille Castiglioni, 1984

**The ingenious counterweight
system solves that perennial
lid problem.**

SLEEK
Achille Castiglioni,
1962 and 1996

**These colorful plastic
mayonnaise spoons, with
their long handles and
small scooped bowls,
solve another problem—
how to get that last blob
of mayonnaise from the
bottom of the jar.**

DRY
Achille Castiglioni, 1982

**Castiglioni designed Alessi's
first cutlery set, Dry.
The pieces are distinguished
by their neat, nipped-in
necks and flat handles.
The collection of accessories
includes a mocha coffee
spoon, a long drink spoon,
and a salad set.**

PROVOCATIVE and paradoxical, Alessandro Mendini is regularly to be found at the eye of a design storm. In the 1970s he was co-founder of the radical design group Global Tools, and then championed the concept of "banal design" in a move to question attitudes toward the notions of taste, value, and function. He has always stressed the importance of individual thought.

Mendini and Alessi first worked together at the end of the 1970s. Mendini's refreshing anarchy, at a time when questioning the supremacy of the Modernists was almost heresy, appealed to Alberto Alessi's growing interest in applying philosophical thought to the nature and role of objects and industry.

The designer's first project was the book and exhibition, *Domestic Landscape*. The work was key to shaping the company's future and, according to Mendini, "initiated the company's process of self-awareness." The study proposed a framework for expansion that included the possibility of working with a range of collaborators and expressed the desire to plot the company on the cultural map of contemporary design. Three goals were pursued: an examination of the history of the household object, the questioning of the company's role as an industrial manufacturer, and the creation of an Alessi style that would incorporate families of objects. These remain the company's main preoccupations.

Alessi and Mendini are great friends as well as colleagues and have established a dynamic relationship. Mendini describes their work as a "continuous sequence, albeit not very frequent, of conversations, reasoning, and general ideas, that gradually focus themselves in projects, contacts, objects, and exhibitions."

As well as his consultancy work, Mendini has also designed for Alessi—his most successful project to date has been the playful Anna G corkscrew designed in 1994.

ANNA G
Alessandro Mendini, 1994

With her colorful party dress and smiling face, the Anna G corkscrew *(below and opposite)* has been a great success. Such is her popularity that she has become a company icon—a monumental Anna G figure now stands guard outside the Alessi warehouse in Crusinallo.

PEYRANO
Alessandro Mendini, 1990

"A chocolate box is a place of hidden delights," says Mendini, "but as I have a penchant for melancholy, this box is also like the mysterious face of a sleeping person." The lid is lifted by the sleeper's "nose."

Working closely with Alberto Alessi, Mendini has played a pivotal role in developing the Alessi philosophy. He often uses conceptual diagrams or "galaxies" as a way of mapping out Alessi's complex interrelationship of ideas and processes, and to crystallize new thoughts.

23

QUINTESSENTIALLY ALESSI in spirit, the Tea and Coffee Piazza was born of the urge to experiment, to question, and to contribute to the new.

Following the success of the *Domestic Landscape* project *(see page 22)*, Alberto Alessi and Alessandro Mendini were convinced that Italian design was in need of a fillip. There was a distinct feeling that the famous "bel design"— the flourishing of Italian creativity that began in the 1950s—was exhausted and required a successor. The idealistic Alberto Alessi recalls his motivation: "Ours was an attempt to make a major contribution to the history of design in the '80s." Chosen to take part in the Tea and Coffee Piazza were ten architects, none of whom had previously worked in industrial design: Michael Graves, Oscar Tusquets, Hans Hollein, Charles Jencks, Paolo Portoghesi, Richard Meier, Robert Venturi, Stanley Tigerman, Aldo Rossi, and Kazumasa Yamashita. (Mendini himself also participated.) The architects were asked to consider the archetype of the tea and coffee service and its relationship to the realm of architecture, and also to examine their own ideas about architecture (this was in the heat of the debate about Neo- and Post-Modernism). The theme of the piazza, with its role as urban hub and center of cultural exchange, was a key design element.

The participants were given the option of designing for mass production or for more limited handcrafted manufacture. While they all started out aiming for mass production, the designs proved too complex and were in due course handcrafted in silver and produced in limited editions of 99, each numbered and signed. As with all metaprojects, the designers were encouraged to experiment with materials and production processes. They reassessed the shapes, forms, and indeed the very concept of a tea and coffee set.

Not surprisingly the gestation process took several years. The freedom afforded the architects

TEA AND COFFEE
PIAZZA
Michael Graves, 1983

With a Post-Modern flourish, Michael Graves loads his Tea and Coffee Piazza with the columns and capitals of classical architecture —and then adds jolly plastic handles and finials. The delightful designs led to Graves' subsequent commission to design an Alessi kettle and then an entire family of kitchen and tableware.

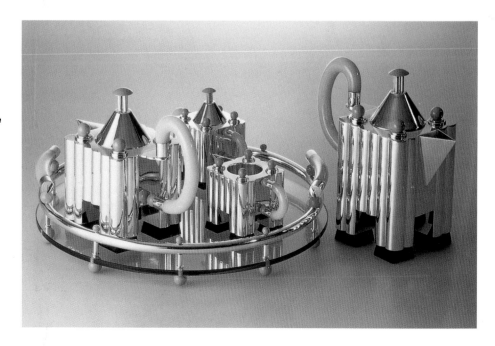

TEA AND COFFEE PIAZZA
Aldo Rossi, 1983

Rossi's interpretation of the brief was to produce designs that are both architectonic and anthropomorphic— the vessels are reminiscent of medieval town elders with long gowns and towering hats.

25

took many of them by surprise. "The service had few if any design restrictions. We never discussed the cost of materials or even issues of fabrication. Essentially, we enjoyed carte blanche," recalls Michael Graves.

The result was a sequence of extraordinarily beautiful and exquisitely made designs. Meier collided cubic geometry with rounded forms, Portoghesi constructed a small townscape of interlocking hexagonal containers, Graves produced a set of miniature Post-Modern "buildings," Hollein chose as his piazza the flat bed of an aircraft carrier, and Tigerman surreally deployed ears for handles and lips for spouts.

The work sent out ripples that were felt far beyond the bounds of Alessi. In the years that followed there was a distinct trend among other manufacturers toward strongly expressive designs; other companies, too, staged their own versions of the metaproject and architects were more frequently asked to design household wares. For Alessi, the project generated considerable publicity; the keeping of such esteemed company brought kudos and confidence; a tour of American museums and galleries raised the international Alessi profile; and it brought Graves and Rossi into the circle of maestros. "The Piazza gave us a definitive international presence," recalls Alberto. It also provided the springboard for the Officina label, launched in 1983. Freed from the constraints imposed by mass production, Officina Alessi is the experimental branch of the company, able to test new ideas in limited, often handmade, production.

TEA AND
COFFEE PIAZZA
Robert Venturi, 1983

Venturi's bulbous forms with inlaid gold detailing (left) **recall tea and coffee sets from a gracious age. They have a distinctive Art Deco air.**

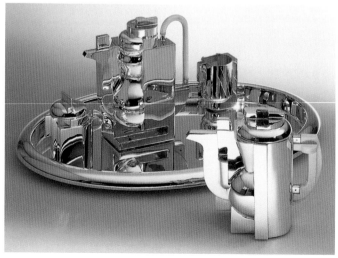

TEA AND
COFFEE PIAZZA
Richard Meier, 1983

The exciting collision of hard-edged cubic geometry and soft, rounded shapes make Richard Meier's tea and coffee set (right) **dazzling to behold.**

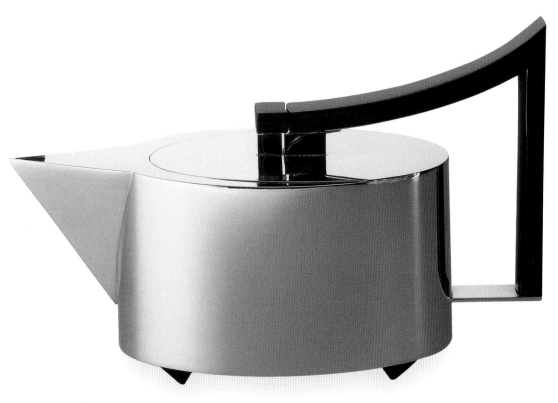

In a very individual
interpretation of the brief,
Hans Hollein made his
piazza into the deck of
an aircraft carrier. His
tea- and coffeepots pay
homage to the sleek shapes
of aircraft and ships.

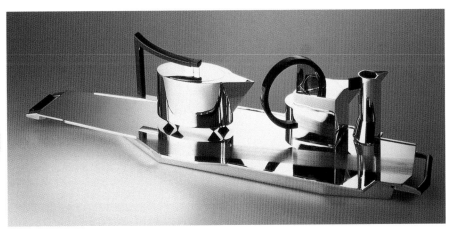

THE LOVE OF CLASSICAL architectural forms is present in all of Aldo Rossi's work, whether he is designing a floating theater in Venice or a coffeepot. His Tea and Coffee Piazza set (see page 25), which first drew him into collaboration with Alessi, is typically architectonic. Indeed, it has a distinctly formal and urban elegance—the conical-topped tea- and coffeepots are housed in their impressive pedimented glass chamber complete with clock pinned outside and, on top, an outstretched flag.

It was this set of designs that Alberto Alessi asked Rossi to expand on and develop for the commercial market. Initially Rossi worked on his La Conica espresso coffeemaker for the upmarket Officina Alessi label. This was to be the first of a series of coffeemakers and cafetières that engrossed the designer for a decade.

The Milan-born Rossi is well known for his singlemindedness in approaching such design subjects: "It is impossible to think without having an obsession; and it is impossible to create anything imaginative unless the foundation is rigorous, indisputable, and repetitive," he says. Alberto Alessi was immediately fascinated with Rossi's method of working—it was quite unlike the process of negotiation he was accustomed to with industrial designers. "Aldo had a way of dealing with the technicians that was totally different from anything we had experienced up until then," recalls Alessi. "He did a few sketches, then he presented them to us and waited for the technicians to make their observations, and sometimes important corrections." When once asked to submit "proper" design drawings, the usually unruffled Rossi exploded, saying that if Alessi wanted such drawings they should work with technical draftsmen.

The approach to any project is always considered and measured, and once Rossi's researches are complete he looks for a strong idea to answer what is asked of him. "Once it is

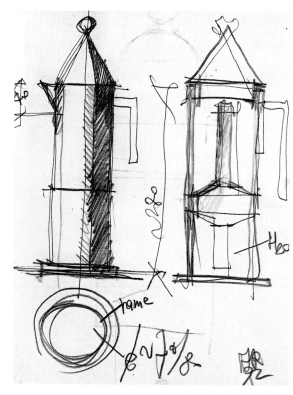

L A   C O N I C A
I L   C O N I C O
Aldo Rossi, 1984 and 1986

Aldo Rossi's decade of coffeepot designs for Alessi began with La Conica (this page). **In common with many of Rossi's designs for household objects, the triple-section pot is strongly architectural. Once he has conceived the design, Rossi's sketches are confidently and rapidly executed. (The power of his initial concept is demonstrated by seeing early sketches alongside the finished article.) Soon after completing work on the coffeepot, he devised Il Conico** (opposite)**, a perfectly conical stainless steel kettle.**

found, if it is really strong, it will be able to survive all the modifications demanded by the technicians," observes Alberto Alessi. Paradoxically, he has found it "a lot easier and stress-free for our technicians to work with architects rather than designers."

The pert Conica coffeepot (1984) emerged as the first of the Rossi series. The three-part towerlike design has its cylindrical body sitting on a slightly protruding flat copper base. Two years later it was the turn of Il Conico, a perfectly conical stainless steel kettle whose body follows exactly the steeply inclined lines of the lid right down to its broad circular base. Then, for the mainstream Alessi catalog, came the elegant cafetière with its body wrapped round with what might be a metal colonnade with its fluting shown in light and shade, and, in 1989, the hugely successful, competitively priced aluminum La Cupola espresso coffeemaker. As the name suggests, the latter once again assembled various architectural elements—the cylindrical body this time capped with a perfect dome that might have been borrowed from Florence Cathedral. More recently, in 1993, Rossi produced the Ottagono—an octagonal version of his Conica in cast-aluminum.

Another of Rossi's highly successful series of ideas is the Momento. This simple timepiece, with a broad flat rim framing the face bearing clear Arabic numerals, first appeared as a wristwatch. It was transformed into a pocket watch and then a wall clock. Rossi is fascinated by the clock and the passage of time. Because he sees them as inextricably linked to architecture, he always tries to incorporate a clock into his building designs, even when they are at the reduced scale of his Tea and Coffee Piazza.

MOMENTO
Aldo Rossi, 1987

Fascinated by time and by clocks, Rossi relished the opportunity to design a watch for Alessi (left). **The simplicity of the timepiece, with its broad, flat metal rim and clear Arabic numerals, has made it an eminently collectable object. The design has a surprising twist—the watch body can be removed from its strap and set into a fob and chain.**

LA CUPOLA
Aldo Rossi, 1989

In a further development of his architectural explorations of the coffeepot, Rossi has designed the La Cupola espresso maker with a handsome dome replacing the earlier cone shapes. First appearing in 1989, the competitively priced aluminum La Cupola has been highly successful. The pot is also made with a colored silicone resin finish *(opposite).*

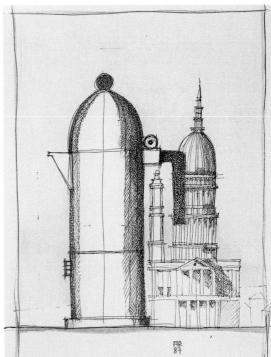

JUST AS IT CEMENTED Aldo Rossi's relationship with Alessi, the Tea and Coffee Piazza also introduced the American architect Michael Graves as a maestro. His charming and witty architectural forms for this service reflect the playfulness of his full-scale buildings. Whether imposing (such as the colorful Public Services Building in Portland, Oregon, with its vast multi-story pilasters) or flamboyant (for example his Disneyworld hotels with their massive animals perched on top), Graves' buildings enchant the onlooker and have won him wide popular approbation.

"Perhaps like no other designer I worked with in the 80s, Graves has shown that he is able to fascinate the general public," says Alberto Alessi. "His gift is an incredible capacity to tune in to public taste—it appears to be a natural instinct." The Kettle with a Bird-shaped Whistle (1985) has been a huge commercial success. The second of the Alessi designer kettles, it sold particularly well in North America and awakened the American public to the Alessi label.

The kettle was a very different style of project from the Tea and Coffee Piazza—it was intended for the main Alessi catalog and so had to be mass produced at a relatively low cost. "Such distinction between projects is representative of Alessi's clarity of intention and purpose in the conception of its work," says Graves.

The architect recalls the initial design brief and work process: "It began with books that Alessi had compiled, books that provided a visual history of the tea kettle, with the purpose of avoiding design problems. We were asked to design a kettle whose body was formed in such a way that it could accept and maintain a large volume of water at its base, nearest the flame. The handle was not to extend over the pot's side, so it would not be exposed to the direct heat of the cooking surface." The result was the now-familiar form of squat circular cone with metal loop

KETTLE WITH A BIRD-SHAPED WHISTLE
Michael Graves, 1985

Adding to the famous series of Alessi kettles, this simple and highly practical form is given a sturdy bright blue plastic handle and is completed with the delightful bird-shaped whistle. Although unmistakably modern, it echoes its ancestors with a ring of raised dots just above the base, reminding us of the rivets once used to secure base to body. The rivet pattern has become a trademark of the extensive Graves family of kitchen and tableware. The kettle above is given a silicone resin matte black finish, while below it has the glossy finish of stainless steel.

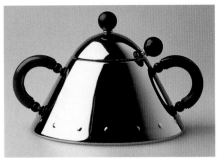

Following on from the Kettle with a Bird-shaped Whistle, Graves used a scaled-down version of the body shape for this sugar bowl.

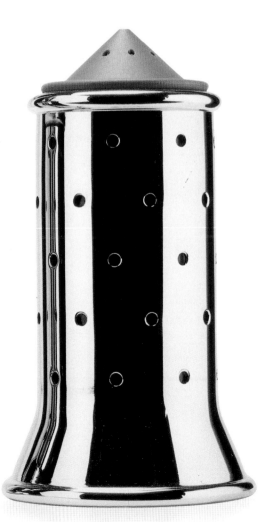

GRAVES FAMILY
Michael Graves, 1993

The Graves Family rapidly developed, spawning a huge range of items including this charming corkscrew (above) **with its distinctive plastic wing-shaped handles. The handles and rivets reappear in the salt and pepper set** (right)**. These appealing shapes have a cartoonlike quality that is part of the American architect's trademark wit and playfulness.**

GRAVES FAMILY
Michael Graves, 1991

The enchanting simplicity of the designs continues with sturdy pitchers and trays. The pitcher above is given a gray silicone resin finish, and is also made in stainless steel.

handle, colorful plastic grip, and tiny plastic bird poised for flight from the kettle's spout. Just above the kettle's base a decorative band of tiny domes alludes to the notion that in ancient times this sort of vessel might have been held together with rivets. This hugely popular object clearly delighted buyers.

The whimsical whistling kettle was rapidly followed by an ever-growing Graves "family" of kitchen products. A cream pitcher, sugar bowl, pepper mill, corkscrew, and tray all burst onto the shelves with enormous energy, looking for all the world as if they'd jumped straight out of a cartoon. The stainless steel bodies, with their trademark rivet decoration, are complemented by primary blue and red handles and lids.

In addition to these playful objects came the slightly more serious square-grid pattern cafetière with matching cup and saucer and mug. To acknowledge the family bloodline, the raised dots appear again. And in their most subtle incarnation they can be spotted on the tray of the Graves condiment set. Once again borrowing an architectural theme, the main glass elements resemble sturdy, ridged columns and are topped with neat cupolas.

At his most architectural, Graves has designed two handsome clocks for Alessi. "I was interested in exploring the well-established tradition of seeing artifacts as miniature architecture," explains Graves. Sure enough, the Mantel Clock of 1988 has its square face set in a block with a projecting cornice; the whole is supported on a quartet of pilotis. His pear wood Time Keeper of four years later also pays homage to its architectural roots, with a classical column formation of base, shaft, and entablature. In total contrast is his Kitchen Clock, which returns to the playfulness of his family of kitchen objects and even features on its hands the tiny birds which appear on the kettle spout.

GRAVES FAMILY
Michael Graves, 1993

An open lattice-work of stainless steel, again with the rivet pattern, is explored on mugs and cups and saucers.

KITCHEN CLOCK
MANTEL CLOCK
Michael Graves, 1992 and 1988

The bold, wide-rimmed kitchen clock (above) **echoes the distinctive shape of the chubby handles used in Graves' kitchen and tableware. The flying bird used on the kettle whistle reappears on the clock hands. With the Mantel Clock** (below)**, Graves is at his most architectural, creating a clock that is like a miniature building.**

THIS IS A MIGHTY NAME indeed in the landscape of late 20th-century design. Frenchman Philippe Starck is one of the most prolific and individual of creators, his skills embracing a vast spectrum of design projects from New York hotels to the humble toothbrush. He has worked on apartments at the Elysée Palace for the late President Mitterrand, designed nightclubs, restaurants, chairs, a DIY kit house, and even a pasta shape. Since bursting into the spotlight at the start of the 1980s designer decade, Starck has achieved pop-star status. With his irreverent wit and trademark unkempt, stubble-chinned look, he has provided a welcome alternative to the stereotypical self-consciously minimal "designer" image.

Starck designs are humorous, wild, ironic, and often sexy. He tends to work in creative binges, escaping from his studio for a month at a time to brainstorm and paint and draw. The work is extraordinarily varied—sometimes restrained, sometimes exuberant—but there are recurring motifs such as the sculptural horn shapes, a tendency toward asymmetry and a use of elements borrowed from aeronautical design (his father designed airplanes).

Naturally, Starck's work with Alessi has been varied and full of surprises. The airplane inspired Max le Chinois colander of 1990 was followed by the massively successful Juicy Salif lemon squeezer and the Hot Bertaa kettle. The three-legged arachnid shape of the Juicy Salif had instant and huge appeal—British design guru Sir Terence Conran summed up its attraction saying that "it's intriguing, tactile, and desirable, and even though it squirts juice all over your shirt, it's fun to use."

The curious and daring cast-aluminum Juicy Salif became one of the company's all-time best-selling items. Hot Bertaa, however, failed to weave its charm and capture imaginations. Despite poor sales, Alberto Alessi considers the kettle an important part of the Alessi oeuvre; like other "fiascos" it is important as an indication of what the Alessi customer will and will not like. "I love the kettle, but it is unsaleable," says Alessi. "However it is extremely precious to me as an indication of the borderline that marks the acceptable from the unacceptable."

Plastic is a medium that Starck very much enjoys and his Mister Meumeu Parmesan cheese cellar with grater is a delight. The "cow's head" box even sprouts a pair of horns. The concept is entirely in tune with the times, injecting a refreshing and much-needed touch of the ridiculous into an everyday object.

JUICY SALIF
Philippe Starck, 1989

Starck's first project for Alessi, the Juicy Salif, captured imaginations worldwide. The lemon squeezer pushed design to new limits and instantly became a cult classic.

HOT BERTAA
Philippe Starck, 1990

With the Hot Bertaa kettle, Starck once again produced an original and innovative design. This time, however, he appears to have gone too far—the kettle has earned the status of an Alessi "fiasco."

Starck's irrepressible wit is seen here in the jolly plastic Mister Meumeu Parmesan cheese cellar—the box might be a cubist interpretation of a cow's head and the horns double up as a handle and serving spoon. With the growing desire to display beautiful and unusual objects in the kitchen, this is obviously intended to be kept on the shelf and not locked away in the dark recesses of a cupboard.

MAX LE CHINOIS
Philippe Starck, 1990

This very beautiful and exquisitely made colander, intriguingly named Max le Chinois, bears many of the familiar Starck hallmarks. His fascination with aeronautical forms can be detected in the shape of the basket—reminiscent of an airplane nose cone—and the tiny airplane-wing-like feet on which it is perched.

FAITOO
Philippe Starck, 1996

Where the Shakers hung their furniture on a peg rail, Philippe Starck has devised an entire kitchen battery suspended on hornlike hooks. Plates, bowls, and cutlery form a decorative frieze (above)**, while cooking utensils** (below) **complete the collection.**

The late 1990s have witnessed Starck at his most enigmatic. His Faitoo range is an extraordinary sight—an entire kitchen and tableware battery hanging from a rail. Bowls and cups are asymmetrical; one edge is pulled up and pierced with the oval slit from which they hang. In plates, cutting boards, and crockery the hanging hole is a neat buttonhole.

The concept takes advantage of the malleability of porcelain clay and transforms the look of the material into that of melted plastic. The idea might be an ideal solution to a storage problem in a small space, but more to the point it is utterly original, intriguing, and occasionally humorous—some of the stainless steel implements feature an expressive face, sometimes smiling, sometimes frowning. And in true Starck tradition each item is given a name. For this series they all contain an "oo"—Soossoop is the soup plate, Hooktoo is the rail, and the kitchen fork is called Mangetootoo.

Starck's work confirms Alberto Alessi's conviction that today's consumer is looking for more than pure functionalism. "The design world in recent years has been having a very fruitful time, which seems to show that people like myself are right to see design as one of the most forceful artistic expressions of our time," says Alessi. He continues: "That's why I like Philippe Starck—he is a living example of my theory on design, of my dreams."

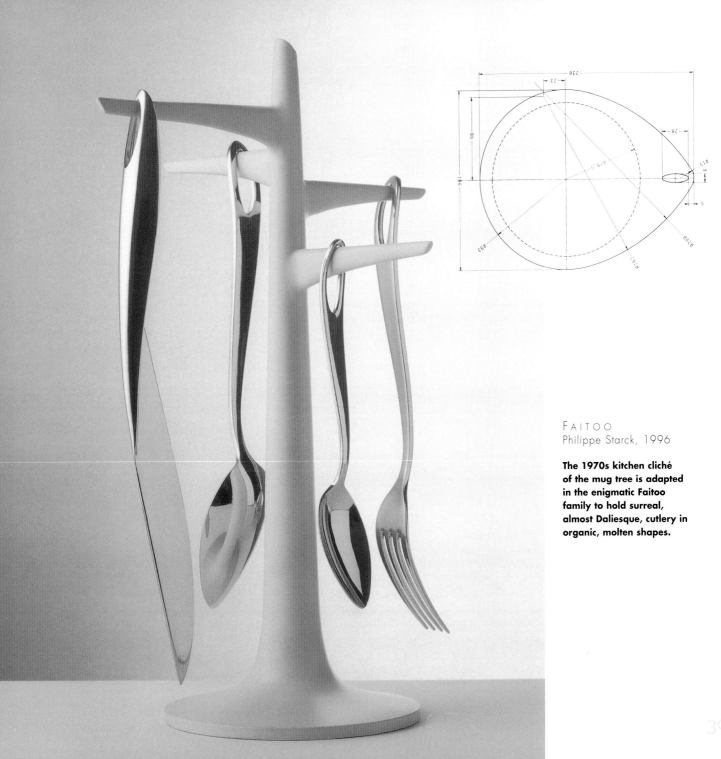

FAITOO
Philippe Starck, 1996

**The 1970s kitchen cliché
of the mug tree is adapted
in the enigmatic Faitoo
family to hold surreal,
almost Daliesque, cutlery in
organic, molten shapes.**

39

THE ESTABLISHED DESIGNER Enzo Mari is among the latest to join in collaboration with Alessi. Having worked with many other great names of Italian manufacturing such as Artemide, Danese, Zanotta, Castelli, and Olivetti, he has become known for his exploratory work in the relationship between craft and industrial production. His work appeals to Alberto Alessi because of its great understatement and precision, and because Mari possesses "a strong moral vision of what design should be." According to Alberto, "one of the key characteristics of his work lies in his attempt to balance a rare openness toward everything the industrial world has to offer, in order to enrich his own personal dialog with existence, with a critical attitude to our consumerist society."

Among Mari's earliest projects for Alessi was the Standard serving cart (1989). Quite unlike the more familiar rectangular models, this deployed a more organic form. Its large oval glass shelves are supported on cast aluminum frames that rotate on a steel spine, and the whole structure is moved on three large wheels. This perfectly illustrates Mari's premise that "the new is designed because what exists is intolerable."

An important aspect of Mari's work for Alessi is the reissue of the designs created in the 1960s for Danese. His early work for the company included games and toys—an early preoccupation of the designer. And in the late 1950s he was also among the first designers to experiment with plastics. A number of his designs for Danese are now produced by Alessi. These include a rectangular tray; a stainless steel ice bucket with an oversize buttonlike lid; a fruit bowl made from a lacy lattice of holes; an intriguing two-way vase, and a lovely learning game of 16 interlocking animals made in expanded polystyrene. Among the latest work originated for Alessi is a playful plastic bread basket and two kitchen colanders (1997).

FARAGLIONI
Enzo Mari, 1972 and 1997

Originally designed for Danese in the 1970s, Enzo Mari's blue and white salt and pepper pots (below and opposite) **are simple and timeless.**

Fascinated by the junction of craftsmanship and mass production, Mari has produced designs of deceptive simplicity. His rectangular tray *(opposite)* **resembles a sheet of paper with folded edges. It is made both in polished stainless steel and in steel coated with colored epoxy resin.**

B R E A D   B A S K E T
Enzo Mari, 1997

Among the latest work originated for Alessi is a playful, brightly colored plastic bread basket. Mari was one of the first desigers to use plastic, back in the 1950s.

Stefano Giovannoni

STEFANO GIOVANNONI runs wild with plastic. His work is the embodiment of what Alberto Alessi describes as "toyfulness" and borrows from the popular culture of cartoons, fast food, television, and advertising. His designs are embraced by the Family Follows Fiction collection (see page 50).

At the start of the 1990s, Alessi's Centro Studi design workshop put forward the idea that there was "a hidden side to the Alessi planet." Many of the existing products, it was suggested, failed to touch our deepest emotions. It was thus decided to explore objects that would answer these needs. A team of designers pursued the idea of "the object as toy," and the use of plastic played a significant part in offering a cheap, versatile, and colorful material.

Giovannoni, who originally studied architecture in Florence, creates designs that are humorous, tender, and often cute. They are conceived to explore that part of our nature that craves expressiveness, joy, and affection. Among his most striking designs is the Merdolino (1993)—any unpleasant or coy aspect of a toilet brush is swept aside in this design that plants a green plastic cactus (the toilet brush handle) in a plastic terracotta-colored pot. In the same year came the Fruit Mama—a stainless steel fruit bowl that sprouts a cactuslike tree in which fruit can be "exhibited" on the table.

The Lilliput salt and pepper set brings a snicker to seasoning—the odd egg-shaped creatures are meant to be fleas. On the base of their feet they have tiny magnets and, if placed at the top of the central metal pole, they will nod their way down to sit on the base. Nutty the Cracker is another zany idea, where you have to turn a squirrel's ears to crack a nut. Delightfully silly, these are designs guaranteed to make you chuckle in the kitchen or at the dining table.

HAPPY SPICES
Stefano Giovannoni, 1997

In the new kitchen the familiar wooden, wall-hung spice rack of the 1970s is redundant. Spices are celebrated by Stefano Giovannoni in his delightful series of plastic containers, resembling tiny flower pots bristling with curious hyper-real plants.

LILLIPUT
Stefano Giovannoni, 1993

Tiny salt and pepper creatures bob their way down the slender metal handle.

FRUIT MAMA
Stefano Giovannoni, 1993

To celebrate the colors and textures of fresh fruit, this unusual fruit bowl (opposite) puts fruit on a podium and turns it into an exhibit.

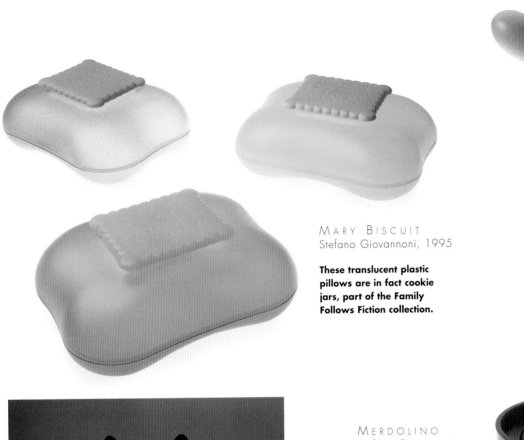

MERDOLINO
Stefano Giovannoni, 1993

The toilet brush is made funny at last with the Merdolino *(right)*. Toilet humor here takes the shape of a terracotta plant pot (in plastic, of course) sprouting a curious green cactus.

43

Guido Venturini

LIKE HIS FELLOW DESIGNER Stefano Giovannoni, Guido Venturini studied architecture at Florence and pushes the idea of fun to its outermost limits. He too has been part of the Family Follows Fiction team *(see page 50)* and creates objects of intrigue.

Venturini's preoccupations are with the idea of the fetish and the darker side of our natures, something he calls "the area of the shadow." He is particularly interested in our most basic forms of expression and is fascinated by the rituals and art of other cultures, especially in Africa.

While his interests lie in the rudimentary and basic, he is attracted to the versatility and color of the very latest plastic technology. His Firebird electronic gas-lighter is positively phallic, while the Gino Zucchino sugar sifter is a mysterious bulbous and tactile creature. The Antonio clothes rack figures are strongmen with a mission to uphold, and the garlic-crushing Nonno di Antonio is curiously and languidly lascivious. Guido Venturini's world is one of witty campness and the double entendre, at the same time laced with a tantalizing edge of the mysterious, the dangerous, and the unknown.

GINO ZUCCHINO
Guido Venturini, 1993

Sweet as sugar, the Gino Zucchino creature with a big grin is an endearing sugar sifter.

ANTONIO
Guido Venturini, 1996

Who better to hold the weight of your overcoat than the Antonio coat hook? The reliable plastic strong man with his bulging biceps takes the strain.

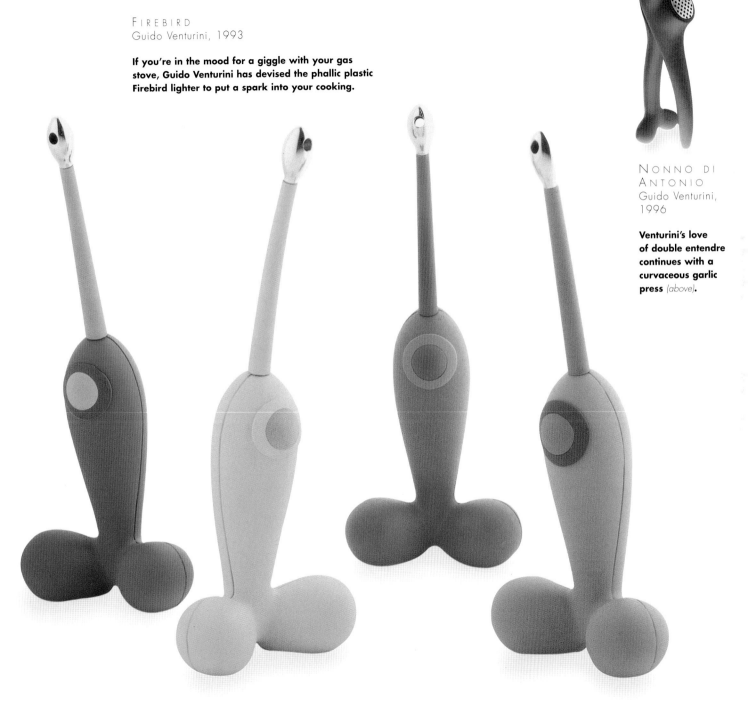

FIREBIRD
Guido Venturini, 1993

If you're in the mood for a giggle with your gas stove, Guido Venturini has devised the phallic plastic Firebird lighter to put a spark into your cooking.

NONNO DI ANTONIO
Guido Venturini, 1996

Venturini's love of double entendre continues with a curvaceous garlic press (above).

THE AVANT-GARDE design duo of King Kong was created by Stefano Giovannoni and Guido Venturini. Their interests lie in popular culture—cartoons, science fiction, celluloid myths, and fashion—but their designs are always laced with poetry and irony. This is all about unabashed childish fun for grown-ups.

The metaproject, which became the Girotondo series, fixed on the cut-out man as its icon. Appealing to the child in all of us, this simple figure was based on the paper chain cut-out that young children learn to make. The name Girotondo appropriately comes from an Italian nursery rhyme that has similar choreography to the English rhyme "Ring-a-Ring-a-Roses." Giovannoni and Venturini decided that their simple dancing men would circle and populate every piece of design. They wanted them to be at once soft and emotional, ironic, and sweet. The body of work is enormous, and encompasses a spectrum of stainless steel household items from round baskets and a cafetière to trays, storage jars, and even refrigerator magnets. As the series developed, the little man was eventually joined by a little woman with pigtails.

The roots of the Girotondo series are buried deep in memories of childhood. We all recall cutting out the simple shapes or dancing hand-in-hand, and the familiar imagery is something we feel safe and comfortable with. "The little man was the result of our search for a strong figurative signal that would immediately appeal to the memory," say the designers. "The formal design of the object was reduced to a minimum. The idea was to treat stainless steel as if it were paper, having the little men circling the edges holding hands and keeping together the objects in the bowl in their own Girotondo." While the King Kong partnership was dissolved in 1993, it has produced two new maestros in the form of Venturini and Giovannoni, whose individual projects continue the "playful" theme.

GIROTONDO
King Kong, 1993

The familiar paper cut-out man provides the central icon of the Girotondo family of tableware, as seen on these metal fruit bowls.

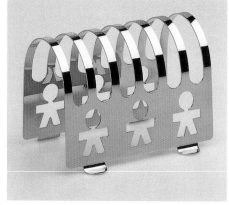

GIROTONDO
King Kong, 1996

The cut-out man is deployed on the entire Girotondo range including this toast holder. The motif may appear frivolous, but it has a serious purpose: to discover the child in all of us and make us feel safe and comfortable.

GIROTONDO
King Kong, 1996

Borrowing the classic cruet set design of Alessi maestro Ettore Sottsass, the King Kong version incorporates the cheeky cut-out man in its base.

GIROTONDO
King Kong, 1990

"Girotondo" is the Italian version of the English rhyme "Ring-a-Ring-a-Roses," a fitting motif to decorate the edge of this tray.

THE MEMORY CONTAINERS metaproject was the first to evolve from the discussions of the Centro Studi. The study and research center was established by Alessi in 1991 to develop contributions to design and object theory and to promote work of young designers.

The Centro Studi, with its team of young designers and board of designers, lecturers, semiologists, and psychologists, embarked on a number of projects that were set out to explore objects and our relationships with them. From these researches came the metaproject called Memory Containers. Initially the project was restricted to women designers under 30 (in an effort to redress Alessi's male-oriented balance), and participants were drawn from all over the world. The technical brief was to work using metals, while the design brief was to explore the rituals and meaning surrounding the serving and offering of food.

One of the objectives was to create a "creole project" that would reflect the meeting of disparate cultures. The resulting designs are wonderfully diverse, ranging from trays and bowls to beautiful lidded pots.

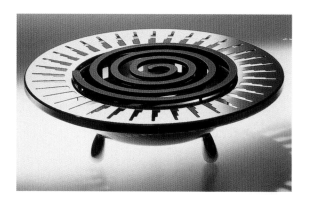

Ovo
Joanna Lyle, 1994

Joanna Lyle's interpretation of the Memory Containers brief resulted in a new slant on traditional "feminine" shapes.

BRASERO
Maria Sanchez, 1992

Celebrating the electric stove ring and framing it in a starburst, Maria Sanchez has devised a highly charged serving platform (opposite).

TRAFIORE LOVE
Marta Sansoni, 1992,
Remo Buti, 1994

Triofore (below left) **and Love** (below right) **add a further new twist to the ritual of offering food.**

HELMUT
Cecilia Cassina, 1992

Cassina's steep-sided bowl experiments with the technical complexities of piercing metal.

THE SECOND metaproject to spring from the Centro Studi, after Memory Containers, was Family Follows Fiction. This is Alessi's quirkiest, weirdest, and wildest design collection and to old Modernist eyes represents a shocking departure for the company. It may have Alessi's conservative fans pleading for the production lines to stop, but it is also the body of work that is exciting the most interest from young designers and buyers. To Alberto Alessi it is one of the most important future directions.

Inspiration was drawn from a number of quarters. The Centro Studi research center had identified that there was a hidden side to the Alessi "planet" and the young designers wanted to explore what this might contain. "The authoritativeness, lucidity, and impact of the products that had been made until then did not quite satisfy our most delicate, tender, intimate demands," says Centro Studi director Laura Polinoro. "We needed new sensual experiences, and new materials to represent our new thoughts. Furthermore, we were aware of being at the end of the millennium, and perhaps even of having come to the end of the word 'design' as it has been used. We felt the need to shake off the restrictions of the past and throw ourselves into the seductive idea of the new century."

Meanwhile, Alberto Alessi was fascinated by the work of psychoanalysts Franco Fornari and D. W. Winnicott. The first developed a Theory of Affective Codes that identified two kinds of meaning present in language: "the state of the day," controlling reason and function, and "the state of the night," bound up with fantasy and emotion. He suggested that our choices in life are almost always ruled by "the state of the night." Winnicott, meanwhile, identified in human existence an unknown zone between dreams and reality, a place half-way between things perceived and things conceived. This he called "the area of transitional phenomena," an

C H R I S T Y
Christopher Dresser,
1864 and 1993

Remarkably, the design for this three-legged sugar bowl (right) **is more than a century old. It belongs to the British designer Christopher Dresser— perhaps one of the very first industrial designers. It is produced in plastic for the Family Follows Fiction collection, and in stainless steel for Archivi** (see page 54)**. The spooky Diabolix bottle opener** (left) **is by Biagio Cisotti.**

P E N G U I N   T E A
Perangelo Caramia,
1993

Part of a small family of penguin-inspired vessels in the Family Follows Fiction series is this Penguin Teapot.

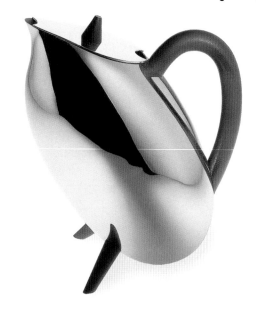

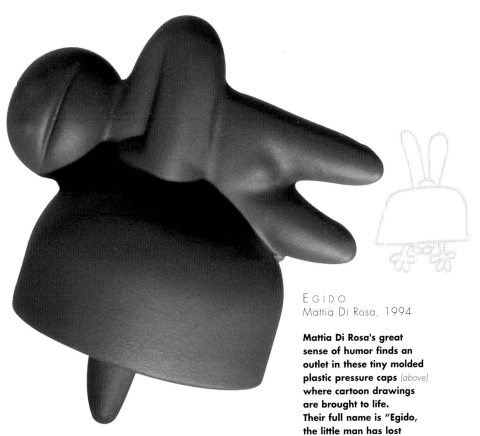

CARLO
Mattia Di Rosa, 1994

Carlo, "a little ghost on the top of a bottle," is a stopper with a difference.

EGIDO
Mattia Di Rosa, 1994

Mattia Di Rosa's great sense of humor finds an outlet in these tiny molded plastic pressure caps *(above)* where cartoon drawings are brought to life. Their full name is "Egido, the little man has lost something."

LUCA
Mattia Di Rosa, 1994

Also called "a little monster eating a napkin," Luca the linen-hungry monster has become an Alessi best-seller.

GIANNI
Mattia Di Rosa, 1994

The irresistible character of Gianni, "a little man holding on tight," never fails to raise a smile.

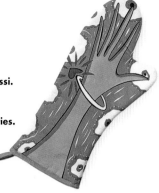

The Comix in the Kitchen textile series is a new departure for Alessi. This brightly colored oven glove forms part of Massimo Giacon's cartoon-style Loving the Alien series.

Also by Giacon are these brightly colored paper napkins—it almost seems a shame to throw them away.

area populated by games, teddy bears, things that remind us of our childhood and safety.

Both of these theories combined to convince Alberto Alessi that in our deepest beings we respond to (and have an urgent need for) uncomplicated and often quite childish objects. "Earlier this century Modernism introduced clean lines and plain surfaces, and everything was cool and orderly," he points out, "but this robbed us of a very basic need for decoration, color, and objects we feel comfortable with and can readily relate to. I think now is the time to re-explore all those emotional aspects of our relationship with objects."

All of this combined to suggest a new metaproject, one that would consider "the object as toy." The title became Family Follows Fiction, an obvious pun on the Modernist mantra Form Follows Function. The designers were to explore beyond aesthetics, style, or culture to devise objects that would touch us deeply. Furthermore, the design team was asked to experiment with plastic in order better to explore the world of color and sensuality in

objects. The resulting wacky collection includes the more established names of Giovannoni, Mendini, Morozzi, and Venturini as well as the delightful cartoonlike characters of Mattia Di Rosa and other up-and-coming designers.

The latest work for the collection is the Comix in the Kitchen series. This is Alessi's first venture into printed fabrics, and includes aprons, oven gloves, and dish towels. A number of designers were commissioned to create designs: Sergio Cascavilla, with his oddball graphics that he calls *"Polle e guai non mancano mai"* ("There will always be chicken and problems"); Massimo Giacon, with his Loving the Alien designs; and the flamboyant Spaniard Javier Mariscal, with Planeta Vivo. The colors are loud and the graphics—featuring friendly aliens, stylized animals and a young urban hero—obviously take their cue from children's cartoons. Like many of the Family Follows Fiction objects, these are items that any confirmed Modernist—wedded to the classic blue-and-white striped butcher's apron—will find deeply puzzling... which is, of course, the whole idea.

Strong colors and dazzling designs are the hallmark of Massimo Giacon's Loving the Alien series, as shown in this striking apron.

PLANETA VIVO
TEA TOWEL
Javier Mariscal, 1997

The enigmatic Spanish designer Javier Mariscal has joined the illustrious Alessi maestros with his energetic Planeta Vivo series of designs which include this dish towel *(opposite)*.

IN ADDITION TO its rigorous pursuit of the future, Alessi has also developed a collection of objects that pay homage to the past. The Archivi collection comprises classic re-editions of some of the great creative moments in modern design history.

The tea and coffee service by German designer Marianne Brandt (1893–1983), one-time leader of the Bauhaus metal workshop, was, in 1985, the first to be produced under this label. Dating from 1924, its simple geometrical forms and lack of adornment must have made it a striking object to behold at the time when the heavy weight of ornate Victorian design hung over Europe. Brandt's work is produced under license from the Bauhaus archive.

Alessi then reissued a 1934 tea service by architect–designer Eliel Saarinen (1873–1950). There followed a large collection of pieces by the British designer Christopher Dresser (1834–1904). Considered by many as the first industrial designer, Dresser's work is often sublime. "He really understood the techniques of metal production," says Alberto Alessi, "so it's not surprising that the round tray and rectangular toast rack lend themselves with the greatest of ease to being produced in stainless steel today." The Archivi collection features some of his more complex works—among them are a square teapot with a hole in its center, a Japanese-influenced soup tureen, and a glass decanter that sits on a stand with three "feet." While strictly a 19th-century designer, Dresser's ideas were clearly ahead of his time; indeed, one of his pieces, a conical bowl supported by three legs with feet, is reproduced in plastic for the Family Follows Fiction collection where it stands alongside designers more than 100 years his junior.

BOMBÉ
Carlo Alessi Anghini, 1945

This classic hotel tea and coffee service, designed by Alberto Alessi's father, also appears under the Archivi label.

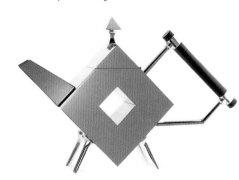

RHOMBOIDAL TEAPOT
Christopher Dresser, 1880 and 1991

Christopher Dresser's powerful and ingenious designs, such as this tea-pot, have a timeless appeal. Inset (top left) **is the three-legged sugar bowl designed by Christopher Dresser in 1864.**

ASHTRAY
Marianne Brandt, 1924 and 1985

Brandt's ashtray with off-center opening and cigarette rest was designed at the Bauhaus. This reissued model is made in stainless steel and brass.

COCKTAIL SHAKER
Sylvia Stave or Marianne
Brandt, 1920s

This cocktail shaker, initially attributed to Brandt but probably by the Swedish designer Sylvia Stave, combines purity of form with ingenious design.

I F THE PAST is nothing without a future, Alessi has wasted no effort in building on its reputation and reinventing itself. The future for Alberto Alessi is always an adventure, and a place where more and better is possible.

Some of the most recent adventures are in producing electronic goods. In the past Alessi has worked with high-profile manufacturers, such as Philips and Thomson Multimedia, but the company is now experimenting with its own lines. One of the latest is Richard Sapper's espresso coffee machine. Borrowing the language of the familiar commercial machine, this domestic model has a sturdy base from which rise the water chamber and coffee grinder. Made of cast aluminum, it is finished in matte gray.

In addition to electronics, Alessi has designed its own contralto saxophone, the Alessofono (1993). The beautiful object has taken Mr Sax's original design and improved some of the famous shortcomings, such as the incredibly difficult fingerings required to produce some notes. The inspiration for tackling such an unusual project as this instrument came from the challenge to improve on an archetypal design and, admits Alberto Alessi, out of sentimentality (his grandfather Giovanni's workshop was involved in the local tradition of producing saxophones). Alberto Alessi was also interested in the saxophone design for philosophical reasons: "It is our belief that the role of industry in our consumer society must be dynamic and creative. We want to prove that the whole world doesn't have to be reduced to standardized, large-scale manufacturing and that good, well done artisanal work can still play a major role."

Personal transport may also be a market where Alessi becomes a player. Already at prototype stage is a neat, foldaway bicycle designed by Richard Sapper. And, stimulated by his frustration with the dullness of the car market, Alberto Alessi has already invited Starck to produce some conceptual designs for his dream car project—the Alessimobile.

D AUPHINE
Sowden Design, 1997

A new departure for Alessi, this chubby, brightly colored plastic calculator adds fun to sums.

P O E
Philippe Starck, 1997

Breaking with the familiar squared-off shape, Starck's radio design borrows something from the phonograph with its amplifying trumpet form, and adds a dash of retro 1950s style.

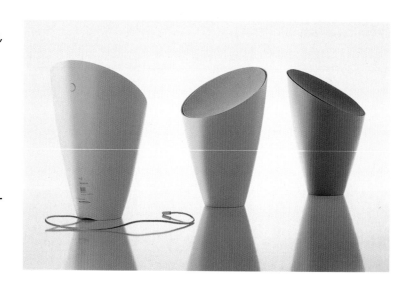

COBAN
Richard Sapper, 1997

Richard Sapper's explorations into the making of a perfect cup of coffee continue with his new espresso machine. Made of cast aluminum, the elegant machine is among Alessi's new adventures into electrical kitchen equipment.

Coo Coo
Philippe Starck, 1997

Once again Starck dispenses with convention to devise a highly original shape for his radio alarm clock, complete with illuminated clock face.

"**H**ere is a glimpse into the future through the eyes of Achille Castiglioni, Norman Foster, Michael Graves, Alessandro Mendini, Aldo Rossi, Ettore Sottsass, Philippe Starck, and Oscar Tusquets. Our world is full of trays and coffeemakers and bowls, and surely there is no need to design and produce more… but when I look into the future I know that we will continue to do so. Why is that? It is as though we are always searching for the new and perfect object, for absolute perfection. I well know that this object doesn't exist, that we cannot reach it, but I continue to be fascinated by the diverse languages of the great designers I work with. I wait with excitement to see their latest ideas—and when there is magic, I know we've done a good job."

Alberto Alessi, April 1997

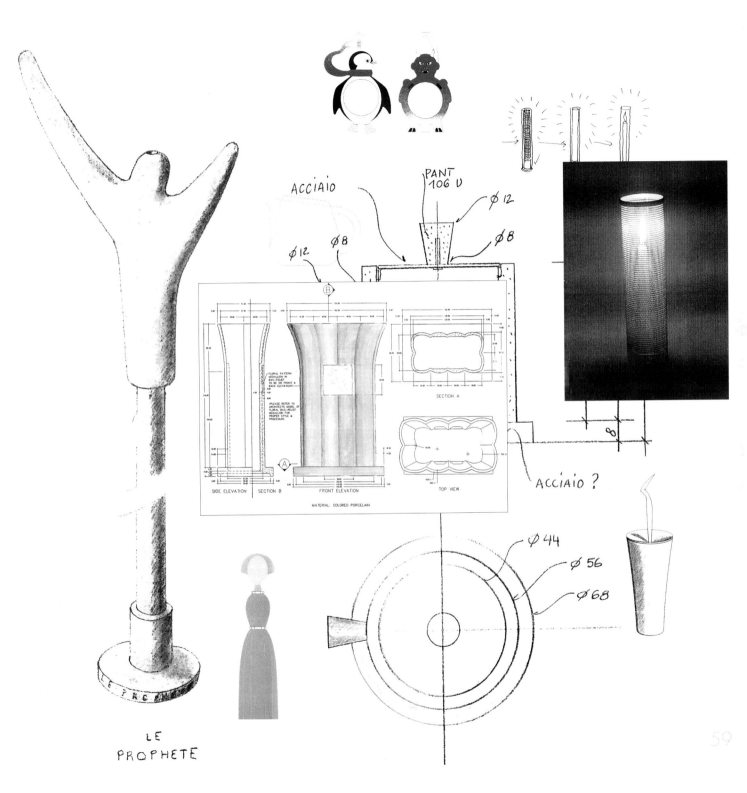

ACCIAIO

PANT
106 U

ϕ12

ϕ8

ϕ12 ϕ8

FLORAL PATTERN
MEDALLION IN
BAS-RELIEF
TO BE ON FRONT &
BACK ELEVATIONS.

PLEASE REFER TO
ARCHITECTS MODEL OF
FLORAL BAS-RELIEF
MEDALLION FOR
PROPER STYLE &
PROCEDURE.

B

SECTION A

A

SIDE ELEVATION   SECTION B   FRONT ELEVATION   TOP VIEW

MATERIAL: COLORED PORCELAIN

ACCIAIO ?

8

ϕ44

ϕ56

ϕ68

LE
PROPHETE

59

1921
Company founded by Giovanni Alessi Anghini in Omegna, northern Italy. Initially a lathe-works and factory working for outside clients, Alessi begins making its own products in 1924.

1928
Company moves to Crusinallo.

1932
Carlo (eldest son of Giovanni Alessi) joins the company after studying industrial design in Novara. Designs numerous objects, including the Bombé tea and coffee service.

1945
In the post-war period Alessi moves from being a craft-based outfit to a large-scale industrial concern. Distribution becomes international, reaching 70 countries within a few years.

1955
Carlo leaves his design activities to become General Manager. Under the guidance of Carlo's brother Ettore, the company begins collaboration with outside designers. Luigi Massoni, Carlo Mazzeri, and Anselmo Vitale are commissioned to design a number of objects, mainly for the hotel and catering trade. Among them is the 870 cocktail shaker, still an Alessi best-seller.

1970
Alberto Alessi joins the company after completing law degree in Milan.

1972
Alberto commissions Ettore Sottsass to design some trays and a condiment set. Sottsass becomes the first Alessi "maestro."

1975
Alberto's brother Michele joins the company.

1977
Richard Sapper is commissioned to design the first Alessi coffeemaker.

1979

The Domestic Landscape exhibition, an investigation into the company's history, is coordinated by Alessandro Mendini, who goes on to become Alessi's general design consultant.

1980

Achille Castiglioni begins collaboration with Alessi. Alessio, the third brother, joins the company.

1983

The Tea and Coffee Piazza project launches the exclusive Officina Alessi label and introduces new famous-name designers to the company.

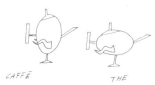

1984

Following their work on the Tea and Coffee Piazza, Aldo Rossi and Michael Graves begin long-term collaborations with Alessi. Stefano, Alberto's cousin, joins the company.

1986

Philippe Starck begins working with Alessi. His first project is the Juicy Salif lemon squeezer.

1989

King Kong, the design duo of Giovannoni and Venturini, launch their Girotondo series.

1990

The design study and research center, Centro Studi, is founded in Milan.

1993

Launch of Family Follows Fiction series.

1997

Enzo Mari is invited to become an Alessi "maestro."

Index

Acknowledgments

The publishers wish to thank Alberto Alessi and Ausilia Fortis at Alessi s.p.a. for their kind cooperation and assistance with all aspects of this project.

Photographic credits:

All photographs courtesy of Il Quadrifoglio, Milan, apart from:

Portrait of Ettore Sottsass (p.14), courtesy Ettore Sottsass
Portrait of Achille Castiglioni (p.20), courtesy Dr. Achille Castiglioni
Portrait of Michael Graves (p.32), courtesy Graves Design
Portrait Enzo Mari (p.40), courtesy Enzo Mari e Associati
Portrait of Stefano Giovannoni (p.42), courtesy Stefano Giovannoni

Endpapers: Conceptual diagrams for Alessi, by Alessandro Mendini.